curiou♀about
FACTORY ROBOTS

BY LELA NARGI

AMICUS LEARNING

What are you

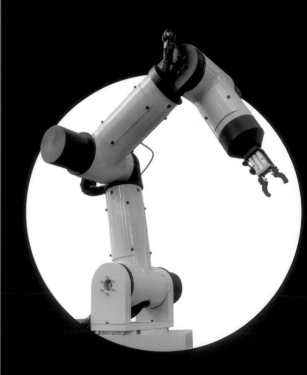

curious about?

CHAPTER THREE

3

Once and Future Robots
PAGE
14

Curious About is published by
Amicus Learning, an imprint of Amicus
P.O. Box 227
Mankato, MN 56002
www.amicuspublishing.us

Editor: Rebecca Glaser
Series and Book Designer: Kathleen Petelinsek
Photo researcher: Omay Ayres

Library of Congress Cataloging-in-Publication Data
Names: Nargi, Lela, author.
Title: Curious about factory robots / by Lela Nargi.
Description: Mankato, MN : Amicus Learning, an imprint of
Amicus, 2024. | Series: Curious about robotics | Includes
bibliographical references and index. | Audience: Ages
5–9 | Audience: Grades K–3 | Summary: "Questions and
answers give kids an understanding about the technology
of factory robots, including why factories need robots and
the types of jobs they do. Includes infographics to support
visual learning and back matter to support research skills,
plus a glossary and index"—Provided by publisher.
Identifiers: LCCN 2023013272 (print) | LCCN 2023013273
(ebook) | ISBN 9781645496502 (library binding) | ISBN
9781681529394 (paperback) | ISBN 9781645496762 (pdf)
Subjects: LCSH: Robots, Industrial—Juvenile literature.
| Robotics—Social aspects—Juvenile literature.
Classification: LCC TS191.8 .N36 2024 (print) | LCC
TS191.8 (ebook) | DDC 670.42/72-dc23/eng/20230330
LC record available at https://lccn.loc.gov/2023013272
LC ebook record available at https://lccn.loc.gov/2023013273

Photos © Alamy/REUTERS/Fabian Bimmer, 7, Science History
Images, 15; iStock/Boris25, 11, PhonlamaiPhoto, Cover,
1; Robots Done Right/FANUC, 11; Shutterstock/Alaettin
YILDIRIM, 2, 4–5, asharkyu, 2, 11, Baloncici, 18, Bigone,
8, Blue Planet Studio, 16–17, Blue Planet Studio, 3, 20–21,
FeelGoodLuck, 19, Kilroy79, 22–23, Marko Aliaksandr, 10,
Nataliya Hora, 8–9, Sarunyu L, 13, wellphoto, 12, Xinhua,
7; Wikimedia Commons/Marc Auledas, 11, Pjwiktor, 11

Printed in China

Why do factories need robots?

A robot is a machine. It may not look like a human. But it can do human tasks on its own. Push! Pull! Lift! Roll! Lots of robots work in factories. They mix paint. They **weld** bikes. Some move apples. Others cap bottles.

Robotic machines can cap bottles much faster than a person could.

Do robots make things I use?

Yes! Have you ever eaten a snack cake? Food factory robots cut sweet layers and then dot them with filling. They swirl cakes with frosting. Yum!

At the LEGO factory, robots stamp out bricks. They stick arms on minifigures. A special robot collects pieces for packing.

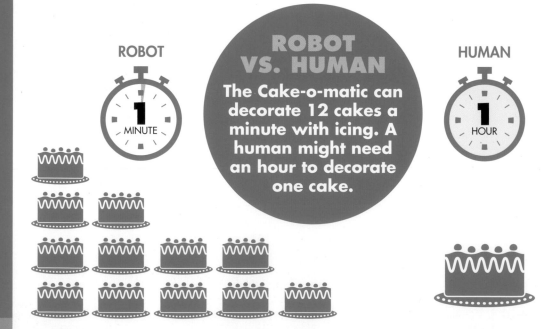

ROBOT

1 MINUTE

ROBOT VS. HUMAN

The Cake-o-matic can decorate 12 cakes a minute with icing. A human might need an hour to decorate one cake.

HUMAN

1 HOUR

A robot picks up LEGO bricks in a production line at the factory.

SHOP TALK

How do robots work?

Robots can lift heavy car parts at an auto factory, but workers are needed to program them.

DID YOU KNOW?
A robot named Godzilla picks up car bodies to paint. They weigh thousands of pounds.

A computer is a robot's brain. Humans type **code** into that brain. This tells a robot how to do its job. A factory might need to make fewer cakes. New codes give new orders to robots. That changes how fast robots do their job.

What motions can robots do?

Some robots have fingers that pinch or peel or plop. Robot hands scoop. Robot arms reach. Robots that look like spiders pick up and put down. One robot spins tiny screws into tiny holes. Another lifts huge tractors. Up. Down. Side to side.

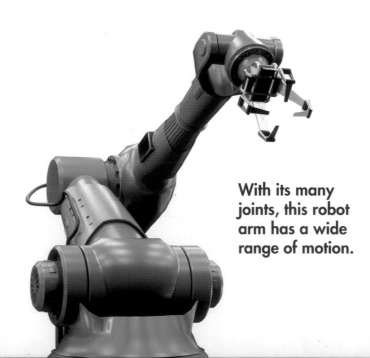

With its many joints, this robot arm has a wide range of motion.

ARTICULATED
MANY JOINTS THAT CAN ROTATE, MOVE UP AND DOWN AND SIDE TO SIDE, SIMILAR TO A HUMAN ARM

CARTESIAN
A SIMPLER ROBOT, CAN ONLY MOVE IN STRAIGHT LINES

DELTA
MOUNTED OVER TOP OF A WORK AREA, FAST AND PRECISE

SPIDER ROBOT
THE JOINTED LEGS OF THIS ROBOT PUT TOGETHER ELECTRONICS, FOOD, AND MEDICAL SUPPLIES

SCARA
VERY PRECISELY PICKS UP AND PUTS DOWN ON AN ASSEMBLY LINE

Can robots see and hear?

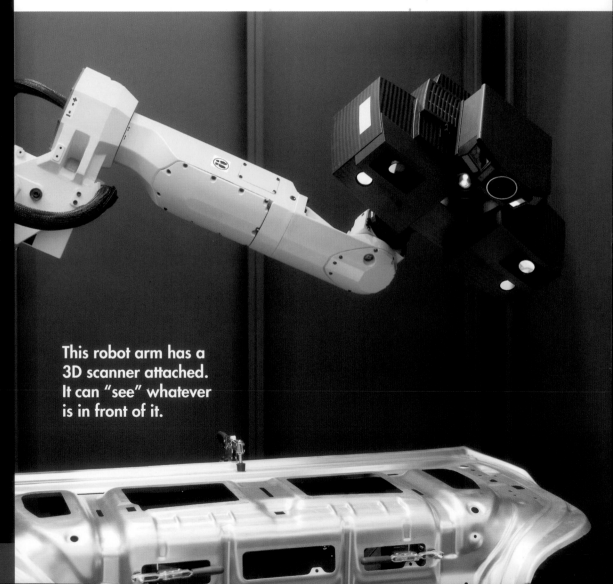

This robot arm has a
3D scanner attached.
It can "see" whatever
is in front of it.

Some robots have cameras. They can "see" where they are going. They don't bump into walls. **Sensors** let robots "feel." They can hold an egg just right. Sensors also help robots hear. This helps them know where they are and what is going on around them.

DID YOU KNOW?
Robots like BB-8 from Star Wars don't have feelings. But artificial intelligence, or AI, makes them act like they do.

Robots in movies often seem to have feelings like humans do.

When were robots invented?

A Greek scientist made a flying bird 3,500 years ago. An Italian artist built a man that could sit and stand 800 years ago. The first talking robot could also blow up balloons. That was in 1939.

DID YOU KNOW?
The first factory robot went to work in 1961. It was named Unimate and it stacked hot metal car parts.

Zadoc Dederick and Isaac Grass invented the "Steam Man" in 1868. It was the first robot in America.

How many robots are there?

More than two million robots work in factories around the world. More are coming. Some people fear they take jobs from humans. Other people say robot jobs are hard and risky. Robots can work faster than humans and are stronger too. Robots don't mess up or get hurt.

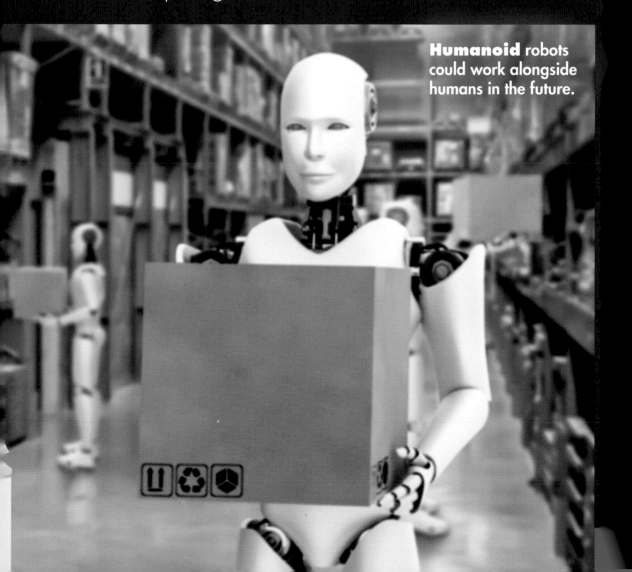

Humanoid robots could work alongside humans in the future.

What will future robots do?

Robots will move a lot more like we do. Robot hands will work as well as human hands. These machines will have parts you can switch to do new tasks. Soon factories will rent costly robots instead of buying them.

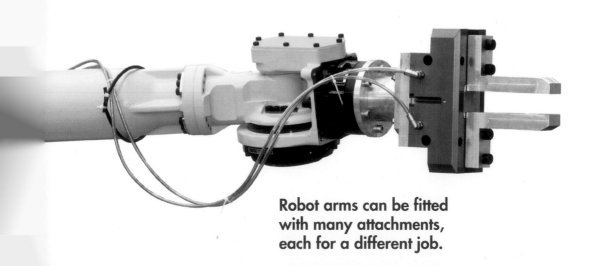

Robot arms can be fitted with many attachments, each for a different job.

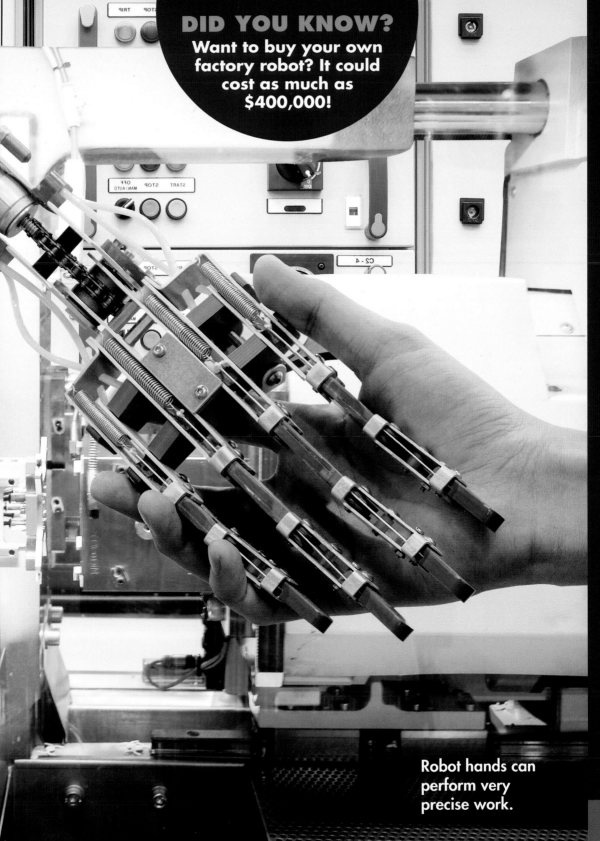

DID YOU KNOW?
Want to buy your own factory robot? It could cost as much as $400,000!

Robot hands can perform very precise work.

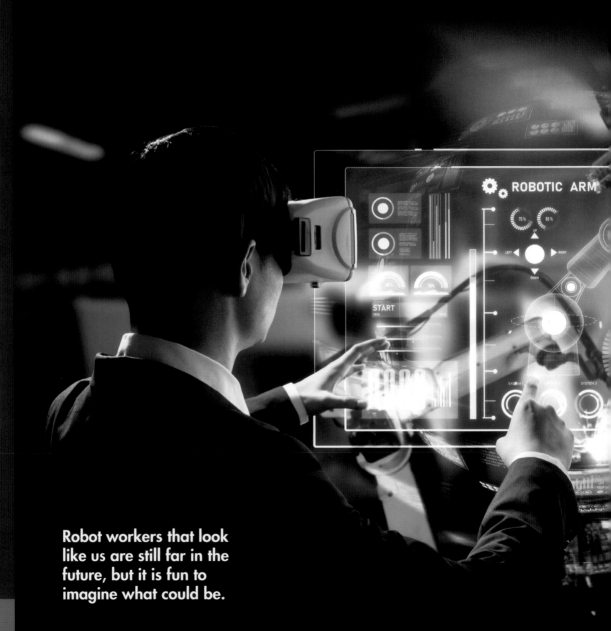

Will real robots act like robots in movies?

Robot workers that look like us are still far in the future, but it is fun to imagine what could be.

Yes! Robots of the future will learn on their own. Some robots will talk and listen. Robots and humans will work side by side in factories. They will decide things as a team. Get ready for better and smarter robot workers. One day, robots and humans might be co-workers!

ASK MORE QUESTIONS

Where can I see factory robots at work?

Can I build my own robot?

Try a BIG QUESTION: What can humans do better than robots?

SEARCH FOR ANSWERS

Search the library catalog or the Internet.
A librarian, teacher, or parent can help you.

Using Keywords
Find the looking glass.

Keywords are the most important words in your question.

If you want to know about:

- Where to watch robots work, type: VISIT ROBOTS
- How to build a robot, type: KIDS BUILD ROBOTS

FIND GOOD SOURCES

Are the sources reliable?
Some sources are better than others. An adult can help you. Here are some good, safe sources.

Books
Machines That Think!: Big Ideas That Changed the World #2
by Don Brown, 2020.

Bots! Robotics Engineering: with Hands-On Makerspace Activities
by Kathy Ceceri, 2019.

Internet Sites
How Robots are Revolutionizing Food Preparation
https://www.youtube.com/watch?v=_GA8xpZL1iU
Watch this video to see how factory robots peel fruit, decorate cakes, and more!

Inside LEGO's Robot Factory Where Toys Get Made
https://www.youtube.com/watch?v=whv-krWnq0g
A newspaper reporter goes behind the scenes at the LEGO factory in this video.

Every effort has been made to ensure that these websites are appropriate for children. However, because of the nature of the Internet, it is impossible to guarantee that these sites will remain active indefinitely or that their contents will not be altered.

SHARE AND TAKE ACTION

Find things built or packed by robots.
Did robots make your breakfast cereal or your toys?

Do you want to program robots someday?
Code.org has free coding lessons. Check it out here:
https://studio.code.org/courses

Draw your own robot.
What job does it do? What neat features does it have?

GLOSSARY

artificial intelligence A computer tool that lets robots learn on their own.

code A set of instructions that humans write into computers.

humanoid Looking and acting like a human.

sensor Something that detects light or movement or sound and responds to it.

weld To join pieces of metal by heating them up and pressing them together.

INDEX

About the Author

Lela Nargi is a journalist and the author of 25 science books for kids. She's a long-time sci-fi fan who has always wondered what it would be like to have a useful robot in the house. What tasks would she most want it to do? Making the bed, definitely. For now, she lives in New York City with a dachshund named Bigs who has probably never wondered about robots at all.